Living in the
Slow Lane

Rob Waring, *Series Editor*

HEINLE
CENGAGE Learning

Australia • Brazil • Japan • Korea • Mexico • Singapore • Spain • United Kingdom • United States

Words to Know

This story is set in the town of
Greve [grɛve], which is in the
region of Tuscany, Italy.

 A Quiet Little Town. Read the paragraph. Then complete the definitions
with the correct underlined word.

    Greve is a quaint little town in northern Italy. Near the center of the large
wine-producing area of Chianti, the village is surrounded by vineyards and is
also famous for its delicious *pecorino* cheese. Despite its size, Greve has
become well known in recent years, largely because its mayor was one of the
founders of the 'Slow City' movement. The principle of the movement is to fight
the negative effects of globalization by creating an atmosphere that allows
people to slow down, relax, and enjoy.

1. the elected head of a town or city's government: _____
2. areas with plants that produce wine grapes: _____
3. when things all over the world become more similar: _____
4. attractive because of being old-fashioned: _____
5. a type of hard Italian cheese made from sheep's milk: _____

vineyards

B The 'Slow City' Movement.

Read the paragraph. Then match each word or phrase with the correct definition.

To qualify as an official member of the Slow City movement, a town must meet Slow City standards for avoiding life in the fast lane. There is a Slow City manifesto that contains 55 criteria grouped into six general categories, including things like 'Hospitality and Community,' and 'Slow City Awareness.' Towns wishing to become Slow Cities are vetted and assessed according to these criteria. In addition, they must offer their own special character, something unique to prevent the world from becoming bland and boring.

1. life in the fast lane _____

2. manifesto _____

3. hospitality _____

4. vet *(verb)* _____

5. bland _____

a. a policy document

b. examine something carefully

c. an expression referring to a fast-paced, high-pressure lifestyle

d. lacking in taste or interest

e. friendly treatment of others, especially by giving food, drink, and a comfortable place to be

The Town of Greve in the Chianti [kianti] Area

pecorino [pɛkərino] **cheese**

The fertile hills between the ancient cities of Florence and Siena in the northern Italian region of Tuscany are exceptionally beautiful. Dotted with old-fashioned houses and old farms, this rolling landscape attracts visitors from around the world and is also the home of some of the world's best-known vineyards. This area, known as Chianti, is one of Italy's most famous wine regions, and a region that has grown wine grapes for centuries.

The richly colored dark grapes that hang on the **vines**[1] that cover these hills are lovingly cared for by the local wine growers. They carefully tend to their vineyards as a way to ensure a good harvest and as part of the well-established wine-growing tradition in the region. Once ready, the grapes are pressed to make one of Italy's most well-known red wines, Chianti. It's a wine that is exported all over the world and enjoyed in homes and restaurants from Rome to New York. Near the center of this wine-producing area, one can find the quaint little town of Greve.

---

[1]**vine:** a type of climbing plant, some of which produce grapes

 CD 3, Track 01

Greve, or 'Greve in Chianti' to give its full name, is a quiet, modest town that has a population of only a few thousand people. Despite its size, it is the regional center for wine trade, as well as a center for the trade of local products. The food market of the town shows the full richness of the local harvest, offering fruits and vegetables from the surrounding countryside in addition to delicious cheeses, olive oil, sausages, and ham. It is truly a place where the quality of life has become evident in the richness of its products.

The town's quaintness, its hospitality, and the **lushness**[2] and diversity of the **undulating**[3] landscape that surrounds it have long attracted tourists and travelers to the region. The current flow of tourism to the area is most often directly related to the **viniculture**,[4] and the various enterprises associated with it, which help to form a highly integrated and productive local economy. It's a busy little town, but while it is full of activity, it is also a village that appreciates tradition—and a place where time is rarely rushed.

---

[2]**lushness:** fertility
[3]**undulating:** rolling
[4]**viniculture:** the growing of grapes for wine

Even on market day, as people walk through the streets, stopping in one place to try the cheese or stopping in another to examine the produce, the mood of the town is distinctively relaxed. Greve is a place where time never seems to be hurried and life often seems more leisurely. Greve's residents sincerely make an effort to spend time with their families and friends, to take pleasure in life, and to really live their lives to the fullest.

Throughout the day, groups of people **stroll**[5] down the streets of the beautiful town, shopping, tasting the produce, enjoying the atmosphere, and conversing with nearly everyone as they go. The town's culture is inherently slow, which makes Greve more than simply slow paced; it makes it, in fact, an official Slow City and one that is quite proud of this special status. Greve is not an exception, a single slow-moving city attempting to save traditional culture; it is part of an organized movement. There are now several of these unusual cities throughout the country of Italy as well as in a number of other countries, too.

_____

[5]**stroll:** walk in a leisurely way; walk slowly

Serene star

FICHI
Italy
€ 6.00

9

Paolo Saturnini[6] is the mayor of Greve and one of the founders of the phenomenon known as 'Slow Cities.' Together with the mayors from three other small Italian towns, Saturnini created the Slow Cities group, which is referred to as *Cittaslow* in Italian, in 1999. Subsequently, several other cities with fewer than 50,000 residents joined the group, making it first a national movement, and later an international one.

The mission of the Slow City movement is to keep the hometowns of its members free from a life in the fast lane. To help accomplish this mission, the group aims to improve the quality of life in smaller towns and villages while resisting the fast-paced, globalized atmosphere that is so often seen in big cities throughout the world. Nowadays, many villages and towns worldwide are applying to join the Slow City movement, but not every town is qualified.

Cities that are interested in joining the movement are first vetted to see if they meet the organization's criteria. Once accepted, they must agree to follow a strict set of detailed clauses within the Slow Cities manifesto to ensure the movement's standards are maintained. The basic idea behind these criteria is to encourage cities to **cherish**[7] what makes their community unique and different. One of the manifesto's criteria is the promotion of local produce and products; another is the encouragement of maintaining cultural identity within the city. Saturnini explains: "Our challenge and our duty, is to try to maintain the soul, the essence, the 'specialness' of Greve in Chianti and all the other Slow Cities."

---

[6]**Paolo Saturnini:** [pɑolo sɑtərnini]
[7]**cherish:** treasure; take care of

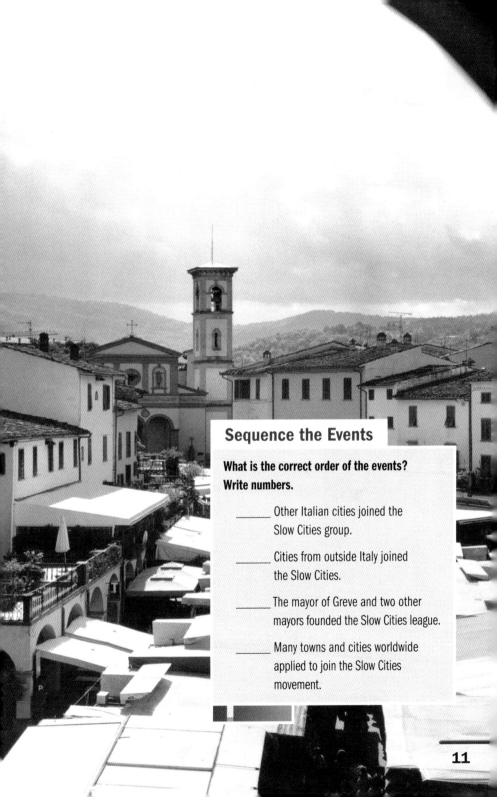

Sequence the Events

What is the correct order of the events?
Write numbers.

_____ Other Italian cities joined the
Slow Cities group.

_____ Cities from outside Italy joined
the Slow Cities.

_____ The mayor of Greve and two other
mayors founded the Slow Cities league.

_____ Many towns and cities worldwide
applied to join the Slow Cities
movement.

Alongside the Slow City movement, another subsidiary movement has developed: the Slow Food movement. This secondary movement is similar to the Slow City movement, and some of the supporting concepts of the two groups overlap. The main difference is that the Slow Food movement differs in focus. Its practitioners aim to preserve the pleasures of good, locally grown, high-quality food. The concept of Slow Food contrasts the tendency for people to eat unhealthy 'fast foods' without restraint, a tendency that seems to have taken hold around the world. Those who follow the Slow Food movement prefer not to turn to easy, low-quality methods of food preparation, and continue to use classic, traditional methods of food preparation.

With the tremendous success of the Slow Food movement in Italy, the movement has now gone international and has more than 80,000 members in over 100 countries worldwide. The enthusiastic response to the notion may be an indication that people around the globe are concerned with the increased popularity of fast food.

This means that in Greve, a quick hamburger for the evening meal isn't the easy answer, but that's no problem here. **Sandro Checcuci**,[8] a resident of Greve, explains that living in a place that values slow food makes it easy to do everything slowly. "It's very nice to live here," he says, "because we have a nice atmosphere, we have nice landscapes, and so, when you have nice things to see, [and] a nice place to live in, it's very easy."

---

[8]**Sandro Checcuci:** [sɑndro kɛkkutʃi]

The Slow Food movement is not limited to the kitchen, either. It also encourages the intrinsic value of taking time to enjoy dining. Around the town of Greve, people everywhere can be seen relaxing and dining together, slowly drinking wine and enjoying their meal. In this region, it's not about efficiency or the rush to get to the television, it's about enjoying time with family and friends, and taking a moment to truly taste how delicious the food is.

While the foods of Greve are wonderfully delicious, such taste does take time and effort to create. To prepare slow food, chefs must appreciate the importance of cooking in a more traditional way and focusing on taste and health. Chef **Salvatore Toscano**[9] is one of those chefs. He used to manage an American-style restaurant in Florence, where he spent his days preparing and serving hamburgers— a symbol of fast food around the world. Then five years ago, he left all that behind and moved to Greve, where he opened a new, different type of restaurant. He now cooks slow food, using fresh local produce, and the results are delicious. Toscano explains what 'living slow' means to him: "It means taking the time, finding the rhythm that lets you live more calmly in a lot of ways, starting, of course, with what you eat." Salvatore even finds the time to come out of his restaurant kitchen and talk to his customers to ask them how they enjoyed the food. Such behavior is often rare in the fast-paced modern world, and it serves as a reminder that dining 'slow' can be an enjoyable experience for everyone involved.

---

[9]**Salvatore Toscano:** [sɑlvatɔre tɔskɑno]

Another local example of slow food can be found in the mountains of **Pistoia**[10] in northern Tuscany. Here, generations of farmers have produced a famous *pecorino* cheese that is said to be delightfully unique. Made from the raw milk of black sheep, the cheese is **hand-molded**[11] twice a day. The process is long and labor-intensive as each cheese is individually pressed and shaped—but the result of all that labor and care can be uniformly delicious. There is often nothing quite like a food that has been prepared by hand rather than mass produced.

The tradition of making hand-molded *pecorino* had been dying out until the Slow Food movement stepped in. The group developed a special promotion to organize the farmers and promote the cheese itself. These days, cheese production is on the increase again, and cheese makers like **Luana Pagliai**[12] have been able to continue making and selling their own *pecorino*. On the farm, they work quickly and carefully to gather the goat's milk using a time-tested technique. After milking the goats, the cheese-making process begins. They first mix the milk with a few special ingredients to make the basic form of cheese. After that, it is molded and packed twice daily until it becomes the magnificent delicacy that has made the region famous. Pagliai explains how the Slow Food movement has really helped her and her product. "It's brought us a kind of **fame**,"[13] she says. "Not everyone knew about our product. The project is getting us noticed."

---

[10]**Pistoia:** [pistɔya]
[11]**hand mold:** mold into a form using one's hands
[12]**Luana Pagliai:** [lwɑnɑ pɑlyaɪ]
[13]**fame:** well-known name or reputation

Slow-Food farmer **Luciano Bertini**[14] sums up the importance of the Slow Food movement in today's fast-paced, **homogenized**[15] world. According to him, it's about making sure that everything in the world doesn't become exactly the same and that the world doesn't become bland and boring. "From Singapore to Macau," he says, "in New York and Rome, you always find the same pizza, the same hamburgers. Slow Food doesn't want this. Slow Food wants the specialness of every product to be respected." For Bertini, the Slow Food movement is about the quality of life, and maintaining the integrity of the local products and atmosphere, rather than rushing to become part of one global movement or another.

Bertini, Saturnini, and all of the other residents of Greve in Chianti and other Slow Cities may just be on to something. They are making a unified effort to maintain a high quality of life, and to prevent the world from becoming bland. While it may seem to be an unusual approach for some, their liberal way of thinking may just be what the world needs. After all, in years to come, they may be able to look back with great satisfaction. They will have been enjoying life while most of the rest of the world has been rushing through it. They will have enjoyed themselves and taken it easy in the slow lane.

---

[14]**Luciano Bertini:** [lutʃano bɛrtini]
[15]**homogenize:** make to look exactly the same as everything else

Infer Meaning

1. What does Bertini mean by "the specialness of every product?" Give examples from the story.

2. What is meant by 'take it easy in the slow lane?' Write a definition.

After You Read

1. Which word on page 4 can be replaced by 'extraordinarily?'
   A. exceptionally
   B. best-known
   C. richly
   D. carefully

2. According to the information on page 7, which of the following is NOT true about Greve?
   A. The population is a few thousand people.
   B. It's a regional center for the trade of local specialties.
   C. The fruit market attracts many tourists.
   D. It is a place where time is never rushed.

3. Which of the following summarizes the last two lines on page 7?
   A. The town is busy, so therefore people don't celebrate tradition.
   B. The town's tradition is to stay busy with activity.
   C. While the town is active, its people don't hurry through their days.
   D. Since the people of the town don't rush time, they are not very active.

4. In paragraph 2 on page 8, people strolling is an example of what?
   A. how residents enjoy the slow pace of life in Greve
   B. how shoppers talk to sellers in the market
   C. how scenic and beautiful Greve is
   D. how Greve became an official Slow City

5. To what does 'it' refer to in paragraph 1 on page 10?
   A. Greve
   B. *Cittaslow*
   C. a mayor
   D. a group of cities

6. Which of the following does NOT describe a Slow City?
   A. a city that cherishes what makes it original
   B. a city that supports what is made and grown locally
   C. a city that has developed a globalized atmosphere
   D. a city that encourages maintaining a cultural identity

7. Which of the following is NOT an appropriate heading for page 13?
   A. Growing Food Movement
   B. Slow Food, High Quality
   C. Traditional Methods Only!
   D. Greve Bans Hamburgers

8. In paragraph 2 on page 14, the word 'intrinsic' describes something:
   A. coherent
   B. inherent
   C. liberal
   D. rigid

9. On page 14, Salvatore Toscano is an example of someone who:
   A. altered his life to follow the Slow Food philosophy
   B. believes that eating Slow Food requires sacrifice
   C. enjoys dining in restaurants
   D. anticipates that all people will change their eating habits

10. Which of the following questions cannot be answered by the information on page 17?
   A. From what animal's milk is *pecorino* cheese made?
   B. What does Luana Pagliai do for a career?
   C. What special ingredients go into *pecorino* cheese?
   D. How was the tradition of making *pecorino* cheese rescued?

11. What opinion does Luciano Bertini express on page 18?
   A. Singapore and Macau lack any forms of regional food.
   B. Uniqueness is an important aspect of food.
   C. Quality of life is more important than the taste of food.
   D. People should be suspicious of global movements.

12. What does the writer probably think about the Slow City and Slow Food movements?
   A. Neither prevents the world from being bland.
   B. Both promote escaping modern work.
   C. Neither is a very liberal philosophy.
   D. Both are positive ways of thinking.

HEINLE Times

SLOW FOOD AND MORE

The Slow Movement is composed of a variety of groups worldwide that advocate paying careful attention to the beauty and pleasure available around us, instead of rushing through life.

Slow Food

The Slow Food movement has been growing slowly but steadily since it was started in 1986. It was developed in response to the opening of a hamburger restaurant near the Spanish Steps in Rome, Italy. Today there are several hundred regional groups in over 100 nations worldwide. In 2008, a group in San Francisco sponsored a Slow Food Nation event where 60,000 people convened. In 2004, the organization opened the University of Gastronomic Sciences in Bra, Italy, to promote awareness of good food and nutrition.

Slow Cities

Like the Slow Food movement, the Slow Cities movement started in Italy. Its followers believe that cities should retain as much of their originality as possible to preserve their beauty and charm. This involves creating strict rules as to where cars can and can't go, and what businesses are allowed to operate in the city. Pedestrians and bicyclists are given priority over motor vehicles, and supermarkets and coffee shops with hundreds of identical stores are not welcome. There are currently 42 Slow Cities in Italy and many more in Germany, Great Britain, Spain, and elsewhere.

Slow Homes

Slow Home is a movement founded by John Brown, a professor of architecture at the University of Calgary in Canada.

Fast Facts about the Slow Food Nation Conference in San Francisco, September, 2008

Duration of the Event	4 days
Farmers Chosen to Participate	60
People Who Tried 'Slow on the Go' Foods	24,000
Bags of Fresh Fruits and Vegetables Sold	35,000
Total People Estimated in Attendance	60,000

SOURCE: http://slowfoodnation.org

He and his group believe that most new houses are being built cheaply and easily, but are unoriginal and boring. Therefore, the Slow Home movement encourages people to avoid standardized housing. According to Professor Brown, it is important for people to learn about design and construction when building a home, and to become involved with making intelligent decisions about the place where they will spend so much of their lives.

Slow Travel

In this age of superhighways and jet planes, some people are talking about slowing down the travel experience.

In 2008, two Swedish tour companies offered 8,000 train trips to various destinations in Europe. Typically, if one were to take a plane, the trips would take two hours on average. Alternatively, the train rides take a day or two. Despite the longer time needed, the program was extremely popular and better for the environment, releasing about 20 percent less harmful gas into the atmosphere than the same trip made by car or plane.

CD 3, Track 02

Word Count: 399
Time: _____

Vocabulary List

bland (3, 18)

cherish (10)

fame (17)

globalization (2, 10)

hand-mold (17)

homogenize (18)

hospitality (3, 7)

life in the fast lane (3, 10)

lushness (7)

manifesto (3, 10)

mayor (2, 10, 11)

pecorino **cheese** (2, 3, 17)

quaint (2, 4, 7)

stroll (8)

undulating (7)

vet (3, 10)

vine (4)

vineyard (2, 4)

viniculture (7)